What Every Catholic Needs To Know About The Eucharist

A Guide for the Liturgical Assembly

Michael Kwatera, OSB

RESOURCE PUBLICATIONS, INC.
San Jose, California

Also in this series: *What Every Catholic Needs to Know about Advent and Christmas; What Every Catholic Needs to Know about Lent, Triduum, and Easter; What Every Catholic Needs to Know about the Bible; What Every Catholic Needs to Know about the Mass*

© 2008 Resource Publications, Inc. All rights reserved. No part of this book may be photocopied or otherwise reproduced without permission from the publisher. For reprint permission, contact:

Reprint Department
Resource Publications, Inc.
160 E. Virginia Street #290
San Jose, CA 95112-5876
(408) 286-8505 voice
(408) 287-8748 fax

Library of Congress Cataloging-in-Publication Data

Kwatera, Michael.
  What every Catholic needs to know about the Eucharist : a guide for the liturgical assembly / Michael Kwatera.
      p. cm.
  Includes bibliographical references.
  ISBN-13: 978-0-89390-680-1 (pbk.)
  ISBN-10: 0-89390-680-8 (pbk.)
  1. Lord's Supper—Catholic Church. 2. Mass. 3. Public worship—Catholic Church. I. Title.
  BX2215.3.K87 2008
  264'.02036—dc22
                                      2008043713

Printed in the United States of America

08 09 10 11 12 | 5 4 3 2 1

Design and production: Kenneth Guentert, The Publishing Pro, LLC
Copyeditor: Kenneth Guentert

Dedicated to

Monsignor Kenneth Hedrick

hospitable friend,
dedicated pastor,
faithful servant of the liturgy:

I thank my God for you.

Contents

Acknowledgments	vii
The Many Passovers of Eucharist	1
Preparing for Our Passover with Christ	3
All Aboard for God's Assembly!	5
What Is the Liturgical Assembly?	6
Who Calls the Assembly?	7
Who Is Called to Participate?	8
What Is the Assembly's Purpose?	9
What Is the Assembly a Sign or Symbol of?	12
God's Word for the Assembly	14
Literary Forms	18
Introductory Rites and Liturgy of the Word	20
Liturgy of the Eucharist: Eucharistic Prayer	24
Liturgy of the Eucharist: Communion Rite	29
Looking for the Perfect Communicant	34
Liturgy of the Eucharist: Sending Forth	36
Come, Holy Spirit	39
Come to the Feast!	41
A Primer on the Real Presence	43
Eucharistic Adoration	49
A Farewell Toast	52
Endnotes	54
Bibliography	55

Acknowledgments

Excerpts from the English translation of *The Roman Missal* © 1973, International Committee on English in the Liturgy, Inc. (ICEL); excerpts from the English translation of *Documents on the Liturgy, 1963-1979: Conciliar, Papal, and Curial Texts* © 1982, ICEL; excerpts from the English translation of *Eucharistic Prayer for Masses for Various Needs and Occasions* © 1994, ICEL; the English translation of *O Sacrum Convivium* from *Holy Communion & Worship of the Eucharist outside Mass* © 1974, ICEL. All rights reserved.

Excerpt from *Mane Nobiscum Domine* © 2004 LIBRERIA EDITRICE VATICANA.

Quote from "Jesus Our Delight" is excerpted from *Lord Hear Our Prayer* compiled by Thomas McNalley, C.S.C. and William G. Storey, D.M.S. Copyright ©1978, 2000 by Ave Maria Press, P.O. Box 428, Notre Dame, Indiana, 46556, www.avemariapress.com. Used with permission of the publisher.

Quote from "Let Us Be Bread" by Thomas Porter, copyright © 1990 by GIA Publications, Inc., 7404 S Mason Ave., Chicago, IL 60638. All rights reserved. Used by permission.

Quote from "Eat This Bread" by Jacques Berthier, copyright © 1978, Ateliers et Presses de Taizé, Taizé Community, France. GIA Publications, Inc., exclusive North American agent. All rights reserved. Used by permission.

Some of the scripture texts in this work are taken from the *New American Bible, with Revised New Testament* © 1986, 1970 Confraternity of Christian Doctrine, Washington, D.C. and are used by permission of the copyright owner. All Rights Reserved. No part of the *New American Bible* may be reproduced in any form without permission in writing from the copyright owner.

New Revised Standard Version Bible: Catholic Edition, © 1989, 1993, Division of Christian Education of the National Council of the Churches of Christ in the United States of America. Used by permission. All rights reserved.

In the event that some source or copyright holder has been overlooked, please send acknowledgment requirements to the editorial director at Resource Publications, Inc.

The Many Passovers of Eucharist

American families celebrate Thanksgiving on the fourth Thursday in November. It is a day for remembering and celebrating some historical events: that first hard winter for the Pilgrims in Plymouth Colony; the Indians helping them to grow corn and escape starvation; and the feast that the thankful Pilgrims gave for the Indians. But Thanksgiving is also a time for remembering and celebrating historical events in our own families (like the birth of a new baby). Thanksgiving is a *history* feast: It invites us to remember and celebrate our *national* history and our *personal* history.

The Jewish people have long celebrated a great history feast of thanksgiving called *Passover*. This national and family feast celebrates the Israelites' deliverance from slavery in Egypt around the year 1250 B.C.E. The directions for celebrating the Passover meal form Holy Thursday's first reading from the book of Exodus. Every year the Israelites remembered and celebrated their deliverance from death in the special foods, words, and songs of the Passover meal.

Jesus was no stranger to the Passover meal and its meaning. He celebrated it many times, the last time with those he numbered as his close friends and helpers. But at the Last Supper, Jesus gave new meaning to the Passover meal. He told his disciples that a *new* exodus was at hand; he was about to accomplish a new deliverance for his people, a deliverance from slavery to sin and death.

As Jesus and his disciples were celebrating the Exodus from Egypt, Jesus was on his way to his own exodus, to the great event of deliverance accomplished in his death and resurrection. But Jesus left his disciples a sign of his self-giving unto death for the forgiveness of sins. When they offered a prayer of blessing over bread and wine in his memory, they would share in his Body and Blood. As they did so, the disciples would become one with him in his passing-over from death to life.

That passing-over was Jesus' return to the Father, who had asked him to give his life in service to all. Jesus often must have felt that his mission was leading to rejection and death, but perhaps at table with his disciples he had the terrifying realization: "It might be tonight!"

Like Jesus as he faced his approaching death, we experience moments where human life is fragile and easily broken: being born, growing up and growing older, being hungry, getting sick, dying. These "passover times" are given to us simply because we are human. They are always with us, or not far from us, and we can't avoid them. We do not ask to be born, for example, and we can't plan exactly how we will die. When we are in the midst of choosing a vocation, being seriously ill, or experiencing deep personal guilt, we know that we can't stand still: We must *pass through* or *pass over* the situation to a different one. That is what Jesus did, and that is why *we* can, too.

Christ comes to us in the basic experiences of human life so that we can pass through or pass over our times of suffering with him. He invites us to fill our passover times with the power of his own passover from death to life. He enters the fragile experiences of our lives and fills them with the saving power of his own dying and rising. Then our lives seem brighter, happier, holier. In all our passover times, we find the strength that comes from Christ's own passover from death to life.

Human life really is one great passover from life to death to eternal life, but there are many mini-passovers in our lives: from sickness to health, brokenness to wholeness, hatred to love, disunity to unity, guilt to forgiveness. The Lord Jesus has given us a special passover moment to strengthen us in our mini-passovers: the *Eucharist*.

The many passovers of human life come together most visibly in our celebration of the Eucharist. It contains all the passovers of human life: the Jewish Passover meal, the Last Supper of Jesus and his disciples, the passover of Jesus from death on the cross to the new life of his resurrection, the memorial feast of his passover in our sharing of his Body and Blood, and the mini-passovers of our daily lives. The Eucharist unites the passover of Jesus and our passovers in a single event.

The Eucharistic celebration itself is a passover time. Here we give thanks for Christ's saving presence in all the other passover times of human life. The Eucharist is the life-giving food of travelers, the nourishment we need as we pass over from sin and death to life with Christ. The Lord loves us too much to let us make this passover alone.

Our sharing in the Eucharist commits us to love one another as Jesus has loved us. It commits us to accompany each other through the sad and happy passover times of human life. It commits us to lay down our lives for each other in service.

Preparing for Our Passover with Christ

The Passover meal, the annual feast commemorating the Israelites' Exodus from Egypt, was near at hand. Jesus' disciples knew it was high time for making the necessary preparations, for Jesus loved to celebrate Passover. So they asked him, "Where do you want us to go and prepare for you to eat the Passover?" (Mk 14:12)[1]

Jesus didn't think too long about his answer: "Go into the city and a man will meet you, carrying a jar of water. Follow him." (Mk 14:13)[2] That man would not be hard to spot because, in the time of

Jesus, it was a woman's task to draw water. This man led the disciples to his house, which was to be the setting for the last Passover meal that Jesus would celebrate with them before his death. And the two disciples, upon finding an upstairs room, spacious, furnished, and all in order, (Mk 14:15)[3] proceeded to get the place ready for the meal. But if all was in order there, as the Gospel says, then maybe the two disciples didn't have too much to do. Certainly those who prepare for our liturgy Sunday after Sunday don't get off so easily.

Today, the question that the disciples asked Jesus is ours to ask: "Where do you want *us* to go and prepare for you to eat the Passover?" Every Sunday, we sit down at the Lord's table to share his sacrificial meal. This sacred feast makes present the whole of Jesus' saving death and resurrection, his paschal mystery. But the "upstairs room" where Jesus wants to share this meal with us is *our hearts*. And there some preparation is needed.

We don't need to cleanse our hearts, because the Blood of Christ has done this already. We know how even a single drop of blood can permanently stain a piece of fabric. But the Blood of Christ marvelously cleanses us from evil and sin.

At the Eucharist, our hearts must be *spacious*. Sometimes our hearts are narrow and exclusive, shutting people out instead of inviting them in. Jesus laid down his life on the cross for all, offering his Father a perfect, unblemished sacrifice for the sins of all humankind. Because the self-offering of Jesus on the cross was for all, *our* self-offering to others in love must extend to all. Here, at the Eucharist, our hearts must be open to everyone, for in our Eucharist, God welcomes everyone.

At the Eucharist, our hearts must be *furnished*. It is God who provides splendid furnishings: "the promised eternal inheritance." (Heb 9:15)[4] This promised inheritance is something we could never earn on our own; it comes to us as the free gift of God. Our glory is the "eternal redemption" (Heb 9:12)[5] achieved by Christ at the cost of his life but given to us without cost. As we accept this promised inheritance, we abandon trust in our works or merits or privileges and place our trust in the mercy of the living God. Nothing in *Better Homes and Gardens* can compete with the glory of those in whom the mercy of God has found a home.

At the Eucharist, our hearts are to be places where *all is in order*. What brings order to our relationship with God and other people is the "new covenant" in Christ's Blood. The sacrificial meal we share is also a *covenant* meal. At every Eucharist we hear Jesus' words: "This is the cup of my blood, the blood of the new and everlasting covenant." A covenant is a solemn pact or agreement that unites those who make the covenant. When we share the eucharistic bread and wine, we are united to the Father, through the love of the Son, in the power of the Holy Spirit. But as we share these holy gifts, we are united to all God's holy people, those who share in this same sacrificial meal and covenant. As we share the one bread and one cup, we become one in the promise of an eternal inheritance.

In the "upstairs room" of our hearts, Jesus spreads a life-giving feast for us in his Body and Blood. There, all the saving power of Jesus' one, unrepeatable sacrifice on the cross becomes ours. There we become sharers, through his sacrificial meal, in his new and eternal covenant, which unites us with God and with each other, both for this life and for everlasting life. Thanks be to God, maker and shaper of hearts that are "spacious, furnished, and all in order," where Jesus rejoices to share his sacred meal with us.

All Aboard for God's Assembly!

If you were a worshipper at Mass before the Second Vatican Council, did you ever think of yourself as part of a liturgical *assembly*? Probably not. Perhaps you thought of yourself as one of the people attending Mass that particular morning, fulfilling your

Sunday obligation as a Catholic. But today, we Catholics are discovering that our Sunday Eucharist makes us part of the assembly.

What Is the Liturgical Assembly?

The liturgical assembly is the church seen, heard, and felt as it worships. The liturgical assembly is the church in miniature, the church at the local level, but no less the church. And thus, the liturgical assembly shows us what the church is meant to be: a gathering place for all-comers, for all believers in Jesus Christ. The assembly is not only those who are distinguished for their high spirituality or religious observance or near-perfect lives. If we were to let only such people in, the assembly would be very small indeed.

A flyer describing Native American powwows has a reminder for worshippers who make up our liturgical assemblies: "Just remember, there are no spectators at a powwow. You're a participant whether you're drumming, dancing or watching the activities." The assembly is the subject, the doer, the actor in every liturgical celebration, not a merely passive spectator or receiver. Such an idea might appear novel, even bold, but restoring the assembly to its place of honor was one of the objectives of the twentieth century liturgical renewal prior to Vatican II.

The renewal of various liturgical ministries exercised by laypersons in the Roman Catholic liturgy (for example, reading the Scriptures and ministering holy communion) has led to an awareness that all special ministries exist to serve the assembly. The present Order of Mass places the assembly at the center of the eucharistic action. The previous Order of Mass in the Missal of Pius V (1570) gave directions for everyone involved in the celebration *except* the assembly. Our assemblies are learning how to claim and exercise their rightful and active role in company with

Christ. There Christ, the chosen priest and acceptable sacrifice on Calvary, makes present his perfect offering of self in word and sacrament. Liturgical ministers of word and sacrament—and those they serve—together form the liturgy's primary minister, the assembly. The selfless service of liturgical ministers helps all the worshippers turn the "I" of self into the "we" of the assembly; thus "Christ is all and in all." (Col 3:11)[6]

Christ's presence in the liturgical assembly gives it great honor and dignity. But the assembly remains the most usual, ordinary, and accessible manifestation of the church. If someone asked you for a glimpse of your parish—to see what your parish is really like—you couldn't do better than bring that person to your Sunday assembly for Eucharist. For at that time and in that place, the church comes to life, life in Christ, most powerfully. The parish assembly for Eucharist is the best homily on what it means to be church. And what a beautiful homily it can be.

Who Calls the Assembly?

Who calls the assembly into being? The same God who calls each person into being, the same God who calls each believer to faith in Christ. The assembly is composed of those who accept an invitation from God. Thus, it becomes *God's* assembly in two senses: it belongs to God, who brings it into being through divine invitation, and it is the meeting of God with God's people. So it was with ancient Israel. God's chosen people knew themselves to be a nation called at their birth to meet God in a desert assembly at Mount Sinai, an assembly for sacrifice and worship. So it is now with the church; we do not assemble on our own initiative (as for a political rally), or spontaneously (as for a football game), but because we have been summoned by God's word.

On the first Pentecost, the Holy Spirit brought many different peoples together to receive God's message of salvation in Christ. Today, the Spirit gathers many believers together every Sunday to celebrate God's saving deeds in Christ. As the *Eucharistic Prayer for Masses for Various Needs and Occasions* declares: "Into [your church] you breathe the power of your Spirit, that in every age your children may be gathered as one." Such is God's loving invitation, an invitation God loves to make over and over again. This invitation brings the church to birth in every time and place, just as it did on Pentecost. This, after all, is fundamentally what the words *ekklesia* in Greek, *ecclesia* in Latin, "church" in English mean; they all mean "called out" by God, gathered together as God's congregation, now and at the end of time. A very ancient liturgical document, the *Didache* or the *Teaching of the Twelve Apostles*, captures this very beautifully as it prays: "Lord, remember your Church and deliver it from all evil; make it perfect in your love and gather it from the four winds, this sanctified Church, into your Kingdom which you have prepared for it, for power and glory are yours through all ages! Amen." (Deiss 76) It is *God's* power, not ours, which gathers the church for *God's* glory, not for our personal glory. But in our assembly for worship, we find the power and glory of God present in Jesus Christ and in us, his baptized sisters and brothers, who share his Spirit.

Who Is Called to Participate?

The assembly is a gathering of people, who look for the mercy of God and find it with each other around the altar, Sunday after Sunday, as they share the Body and Blood of Christ as his sisters and brothers. Such were the ordinary people with whom Jesus sat down to table during his earthly life; such are those with whom he now shares the feast in God's reign in heaven; such are those to whom he now addresses the invitation: "Come to the feast!"

Truly, the assembly is like the wedding banquet in Jesus' parable. (Matt 22:1-14) People in varying states of preparedness (physical, emotional, and spiritual) are ushered by God into the feast. In such a gathering, those who are burdened under the weight of daily living find hope. Participating in the assembly's worship, standing and praying and listening and singing, raises us above our humdrum existence to a new sense of our Christian dignity.

In one sense, the assembly of Christians will always be a "people set apart." Our purpose is not to reject the world as evil and isolate ourselves from it but to receive new energy for bringing Christ's salvation to a world that needs it. Thus, the Sunday assembly is necessary for those who hear the invitation of God and respond to it as fully, consciously, and actively as they can, both within the liturgy and outside it. It is not that we are better or worse than others but that we, for God's own mysterious reasons, have been chosen and gathered by God to acknowledge God and what God is doing in our world and to commit ourselves to God's work. It is God who calls us together; God's initiative precedes our response. The Sunday assembly is a gift from God to which we respond thankfully, eucharistically, with our whole selves, in the Holy Spirit. As we do this, together we become the Body of Christ, worshipping through him, with him, and in him, to God's glory and honor.

What Is the Assembly's Purpose?

The assembly gathers, first of all, for worship as members of the Body of Christ. Our very assembling is our first act of worship. We who worship in the assembly do not do so as a group of pals, or co-workers, or a common interest group; we do so as members of the crucified and risen Lord. We enter our worship space as individuals; we need to be formed into a community. As we pray in the

Eucharistic Prayer for Masses for Various Needs and Occasions: "Gather us now and for ever among the members of your Son, whose body and blood we share."

Like our assembling itself, our worship is first of all *God's* work before it is our work. Our worship is our response to what God has done for us in creation and redemption, our response to what God continues to do for us. All our praise and thanksgiving, our prayers of petition and prayers of contrition, everything we say and sing and do and touch in our worship focuses our attention right where God directs it: to the dying-and-rising way of living that we share with Jesus through his Spirit. In Jesus Christ we find our perfect worship. In opening his hands to the needy, in opening his arms on the cross, he gave himself completely to God. And so must we. Our worship is one with Christ's worship; it makes us his praising, thanking, asking, and repenting sisters and brothers.

All the members of the assembly form the Body of Christ, and all the members render communal worship as the Body of Christ. Thus, the liturgical assembly is not an audience of spectators in a theater or a crowd of fans in a stadium; the assembly for worship has no spectators, only participants. In pre-World War II Germany, the Nazis staged huge political rallies to advance their program. These gatherings were to be the means by which people would lose themselves in an all-consuming cause. So different is the Christian assembly for worship. Through the words and actions of our communal worship, through what we pray and say and sing and share, we do not lose ourselves; rather, we *find* ourselves. We find our true identity as sisters and brothers of Jesus Christ, one with Christ, in the Holy Spirit, for each other.

The assembly offers worship to God within the liturgy. This is its first purpose. But there is a second purpose: The assembly must also offer service to others outside the liturgy. The assembly is two-directional: Its reach extends to God within the liturgy and to the world outside. The two go together because service of God and neighbor went together in the life of Jesus.

Service to the world after the pattern of Jesus is the assembly's task until its Lord returns. Like the larger church it represents, the assembly does not exist for itself but for the world. What we see in the liturgical assembly is the world being transformed by God as the world's Creator and Redeemer wish the world to be transformed. Every eucharistic assembly testifies to God's work in its local part of the world and to God's concern for the whole human race. Yet no assembly is completely free from ways of thinking, speaking, and acting that would close it in on itself and close it off from others. This is less likely to happen if we have embraced an outward mission to others in our part of the world, and if we bring that struggle, that sacrifice, that self-giving with us into our assembly so that we can celebrate and bless and offer our worship and work in company with Christ. We should be uncomfortable, and rightly so, with the idea that we can pray and worship in the assembly and then live our lives outside the assembly as if we were not committed to the Gospel values we proclaim there. How can those who have shared the life-giving gifts of Eucharist in a holy meal deny food and other necessities to the needy?

The assembly's eucharistic response to God's will and work for all people does not end when the Mass is over. Someone has suggested that the most important words of the eucharistic liturgy may be the dismissal: "Go in peace to love and serve the Lord." Or, as the Lutherans like to say with a certain directness: "Go in peace. Serve the Lord." The ultimate eucharistic response of the assembly is to go out as disciples of the Lord Jesus, renewed and refreshed and re-committed to living and being his Body, his presence, in the world. The church gathers to scatter. It gathers to celebrate the Eucharist, then goes out to proclaim the Good News of God's love for all people, to bring the peace and unity experienced in the assembly to those outside, to serve the needs of their sisters and brothers everywhere. All these important, God-given tasks of the

Christian people flow out of their weekly assembly for Eucharist, the source of God's blessing and the power for the task.

What Is the Assembly a Sign or Symbol of?

When we speak of symbol, we are in the realm of looking at one particular thing and seeing many others. For example, when we see our national flag, we glimpse in our mind's eye so many realities: our national identity, our government, memories of our history (both its best and worst aspects), patriotism. When we look at the liturgical assembly, we glimpse what we find in every sacrament: We find an outward sign of inner grace. The assembly lets us see, hear, and touch the saving grace that Jesus Christ gives us through the words and songs, gestures and actions of the Eucharist. When we look at the assembly from the inside, as insiders, we see the Body of Christ alive in our midst, the Body in which we live the life of Christ. The liturgy bids us look beyond *getting* the life of Christ in the sacraments to *becoming* the Christ who is our life.

The assembly signifies the reign of God already begun in this world but still awaiting a future and final fulfillment. The assembly shows us what the reign of God is like, but it also helps bring about that reign of God in the world. The gathering of believers in Jesus Christ is meant to anticipate the day when God's reign will be established in all its fullness, when there will be no more discrimination and division on the basis of gender, race, wealth or religion; when there will be no more poverty, mistrust, or injustice; no more abuse of power and violence. On that final day of the Lord, all things will be subject to Christ, and God will reign over all people in peace—and forever. The liturgical assembly, where we proclaim that Jesus and Jesus alone is Lord, gives us a welcome preview of that day.

The reign of God is already complete in heaven, where the

assembly of angels and saints offer their worship night and day. The earthly assembly shares in the heavenly worship of God. The assembly is a kind of first sketch, a foreshadowing, of the liturgy of the heavenly Jerusalem that we glimpse in the book of Revelation. When we enter the liturgical assembly here on earth, we already participate in the worship of the heavenly assembly. The earthly assembly celebrates the past and present saving deeds of God in Jesus Christ, but it also stands on tiptoe to view God's future. Thus the assembly is not only a sign of the church on earth; it is the anticipation of the church in heaven. The assembly of God's holy ones in heaven begins in our liturgical assemblies here on earth. Aren't you glad that God gives us a lifetime of earthly practice for our heavenly worship?

Both the earthly assembly and the heavenly assembly celebrate life in the reign of God. Thus, what the earthly assembly uses in its worship—its words and songs, its objects and actions—should conform as completely as possible to the beauty, justice, and equality in the heavenly assembly. As we worship in the assembly, we rehearse the words and deeds of our life in Christ that we hope to celebrate for all eternity. Through the liturgy, we experience salvation in a real but incomplete way, and we prepare ourselves to experience the fullness of salvation at the end of time. The "now" and the "not yet" of our salvation in Christ is what we remember and celebrate every time we gather for the Eucharist.

The assembly: God's and ours. The assembly: humanity as it is and as God calls it to be in Christ; the church in miniature; the Body of Christ that needs you and me and all its members; a preview of everlasting salvation in God's heavenly reign. The assembly: God's and ours. See you there!

God's Word for the Assembly

Communication is big business. Advertisers know this. They communicate products. Politicians communicate a public image of themselves, one they want the public to vote for.

How do advertisers, politicians, street vendors, teachers, and preachers communicate with us? One important way is through *words*. We human beings need to communicate with each other through words in the most compelling way; it's a basic part of being human. When there is a failure to communicate in this way, there can be loneliness, suffering, even despair. But words spoken and written and signed can put all these to flight.

Wonder of wonders, our God has the same need to communicate as we do. God has tried to communicate with us from the beginning. God is always trying to communicate with us. In God's loving concern for us, God has chosen to speak to us in ways that we can understand, in human words.

God has tried every means to reveal who God is. God gave us a glimpse of God's own beauty and power in the world that God created, but this was not enough. God spoke to the ancient Israelites through a library of books that expressed God's enduring love: the Hebrew Scriptures. Lastly, God spoke one final Word, a living Word for all time: God's own Son, Jesus Christ, the Word made flesh and living among us. His life, teaching, death, and resurrection are the content, the heart, of the Christian Scriptures.

The Bible says over and over again, in many different ways, that God communicates with us through God's word. The Bible doesn't merely tell us theological truths about the nature and purposes of God. Rather, the Bible is God's way of entering human lives and communicating God's saving presence through God's word. The Bible is the self-communication of God in human words for human beings. Thus, the Bible is a book for everyone to know and read and love.

Our own words can be very personal: They tell others much about us. That's why even close friends don't talk on crowded elevators, for elevators are not places for self-revelation. When we speak words, we are really speaking ourselves. We hope our deeds match our words: We rightly call "hypocrites" those whose deeds don't match their words.

God's words always match God's deeds. In fact, the Bible shows us how God's words *become* God's deeds. Think of how creation springs forth from God's imagination in the book of Genesis: "Let there be light," God says, "and there was light." (Gen 1:3)[7] Remember those shepherds keeping watch over their flocks on the first Christmas Eve? As they head over to Bethlehem to see the baby that the angel told them about, they say to one another: "Let us go to see this *word* that has come to pass." (Luke 2:15)[8] This *word.* That's what the Gospel text literally says, but various translations have the words "thing" or "event." Here we see that God's word and God's deed are one. Throughout the Bible, God's word and God's deed are one inseparable act: sometimes of creation, sometimes of destruction, sometimes of correction and redemption. In all of this, God's word reveals the God who acts in human history, in human lives. *What* God says and *how* God says it tears away something of the veil between God and human beings. God's word in the Scriptures puts us in communication with God, the one who always take the initiative in communicating with us.

The Bible is the written story of God's long, loving conversation with human beings, a conversation that still goes on. The text of the Bible that we Catholics accept as God's holy word is complete; we don't expect another Gospel or letter of St. Paul to turn up under someone's bed. But the Bible as God's conversation with us still goes on. The good stories in the Hebrew Scriptures are not just about people and events of long ago: They are about us today. If you have ever felt yourself backed into a corner like the escaping Israelites at the sea and knew that only God could save you, then their story is your story. If you have ever felt deep joy in the presence of the Lord Jesus, say, at a grand liturgy like the Easter Vigil, then you are one with Peter on the mountain at the transfiguration of Jesus: "Lord, it is good for us to be here!" (Mt 17:4)[9]

The Bible is our story today, God's self-communication to us today, because it is God's way of reaching out to us in love and trust. And the Bible gives the interpretation and meaning of God's efforts to reach out to us. The Bible tells us of God's greatest effort to reach out to us: Jesus Christ, God's Word-made-flesh.

In Jesus Christ, God revealed God's own self most completely. Jesus Christ is the "image of the invisible God," as St. Paul wrote to the Colossians. (1:15)[10] But throughout the entire Bible, God's revelation was the means by which the unknown God became known in a human way. And because of God's self-revelation, we human beings could come to share the life of the unknown God. Revelation is not a thing, like a divine computer program; rather, it is a process of knowing a personal God who wants to be known. Centuries-long growth in coming to know God is reflected in the various books of the Bible themselves. God respected our human limitations in revealing God's own self to us in various ways and at various times. Thus, we have many different voices of the one God in the Scriptures: storyteller, lawgiver, liberator, prophet, lover, poet, visionary, parent, savior.

The Hebrew Scriptures helped Jesus to understand and accept his messianic mission to God's chosen people. Today, the whole Bible helps us to discover and rediscover what it means to live as that people in union with Jesus Christ. The whole Bible helps us to understand and accept God's plan for us, for our church and for the world. The Scriptures give us encouragement, guidance, and hope, just as they did for Jesus. The story of his life, death and resurrection, his paschal mystery, becomes the most important story for us. God's Easter plan for Jesus is God's plan for each of us as we shape our lives according to his words and deeds in the Scriptures.

His dying and rising becomes our story at our baptism, our hope of glory throughout our lives.

The history of God's involvement in this world, in salvation history, came through a particular people of God's special choosing, the Jewish people. They were the "first to hear the word of God," as we recall in one of the solemn intercessions on Good Friday. Certain persons at certain times in their history had deep experiences of God, in which God communicated God's self to them. They put their experiences into writing at God's direction, and they did so with such depth and accuracy that their fellow believers embraced these experiences of God's self-revelation. Throughout the centuries, people of different backgrounds gathered, organized, and edited God's word in their own language, just as God wanted them to do.

Thus, the Bible is really God's word in human language. As God's message, God's self-communication, it is completely divine; as words on a page, as written text, it is completely human. As the word of God and the word of humans, the Bible is unique among all the world's literature. God is the heart of the Bible because the Bible comes from the heart of God. But the word of God comes to us through human hearts and minds and hands. This is what is meant by "biblical inspiration." The Holy Spirit of God breathed God's message into human authors, who then put into writing what God wanted to communicate, and only that. But they had to use the writing skills that any high school student needs when writing a term paper. There is no evidence that the biblical authors spoke or wrote differently from us. God didn't turn the inspired human authors into robots to produce God's words or into secretaries to take God's dictation. God never uses people as robots; thus, when God inspired them to write the books of the Bible, God inspired them as people with different outlooks, skills, and abilities. This helps to explain the differences in the books of the Bible, sometimes within a particular book itself. Sometimes the inspired word of God is poorly written

Hebrew or Greek because God inspired authors who wrote Hebrew or Greek poorly. If God had dictated God's message, the inspired word would not have been poorly written. Here is more evidence that the Bible is not merely human or merely divine, nor partly human and partly divine, but *all* human and *all* divine. It is all human because it was written by human beings, and it is all divine because it was inspired by God. It's like listening to guitar music: You can be sure that both a guitar and a guitarist are producing it. Guitars cannot make music without a player, nor guitar players without guitars, but together they can produce great music. A most marvelous result of divine and human cooperation was the Bible, God's word in human language.

Literary Forms

Whenever we read a book or watch a television program, we have some expectations of what we might get from it. If the book is a whodunit, we expect to be led, not so directly, to the solving of a crime. If the TV program is a comedy, we expect to laugh a lot at the funny situations presented there. All that we can reasonably expect of any book or program, of any work of art or product, is that it live up to the purpose and standard it sets for itself.

The Bible is God's self-communication in human language. But often we find the Bible difficult to understand because of the many different forms of writing it contains. To understand the Bible, we have to know what the human authors meant to say. But knowing what their words mean is not enough; we also have to know the different forms of writing that the various authors are using.

Today, as we read the sports page in the newspaper, we know that a sports column by a highly opinionated commentator is not the same as a straightforward review of last night's game. The purpose of each kind of writing is different. Similarly, the people of biblical times understood the author's words because they recognized the form of writing and they understood the symbolic value of such things as colors and numbers. Recognizing such literary techniques is part of our Catholic approach to interpreting the Bible, and it can keep us from falling into fundamentalism when we read a book like Genesis or Revelation.

The forms of writing in the Bible are many: legal documents, court histories, political speeches, sermons, prayers, contracts, lists of ancestors, narratives, legends, poetry, proverbs, folklore, prophecy, parables, epics, gospels, letters. Many of these forms of writing are found in the Scripture readings assigned to the Sunday, feast day, or weekday Eucharist. The purpose of each form is the key to understanding and receiving God's message, God's truth, in that piece of writing. *God's truth.* The Bible is true, but it gives us God's truth in a human document. The truth in the Bible is not in the language itself because our human words are limited, imperfect, and subject to change in use and meaning over time. Words are often inadequate to express a human truth like the love between husband and wife. And it's simply impossible to define God in words. Biblical truth is not even fully expressed in Scripture's many literary forms because they are only the means by which God's message reaches us. Biblical truth is found chiefly in the intention of the author; that is, what a human author inspired by God wants to communicate about God. Biblical truth is the message that God wants us to know and understand. That message, no matter in what form it comes, is God's own message, God's self revealed in human words. The authors of the various books of the Bible were all trying to communicate one great idea: that God calls a people; that God wants to help and care for them, even when they stray; that God asks this people to respond to God in love, freely and generously. In all of this, we find that God's word of love for us is God's deed of love. Father William Heidt, O.S.B. has said: "Scripture is the map which outlines the way by which [God] wants us to know, love and serve [God]." That is why Scripture plays such a necessary and important role at Sunday Eucharist.

Introductory Rites and Liturgy of the Word

Around the year 150, a philosopher-turned-Christian named Justin wrote his First Apology, a kind of open letter to the Roman Emperor and Roman Senate defending the Christian faith. In describing the celebration of the Eucharist, he noted that "on the day named after the sun, all who live in city or countryside assemble. The memoirs of the apostles or the writings of the prophets are read for as long as time allows." (Deiss 93) Probably the reader read from the Gospels or the prophets for quite a long time while the assembled Christians waited for everyone to arrive for the prayer over the bread and wine and the sharing of communion.

The Eucharist starts to commence when the people *gather*, not when the priest and other liturgical ministers come down the aisle. The Entrance Song helps to unify the minds and hearts of the worshippers once they have gathered. Through the entrance procession and the music that accompanies it, all are invited to become one in the words and actions of worship.

The sign of the cross proclaims the Trinitarian basis of our Christian faith and our Christian worship. This holy gesture deserves to be large and slowly made, so that it can take in our whole self.

We like to be greeted when we enter someone's home, and the priest's liturgical greeting intensifies the Lord's presence and the assembly's unity that were formed during the entrance procession. The priest extends his hands wide in an inclusive gesture of welcome.

The words of introduction to the liturgy, usually given by the priest or deacon, help the assembly to focus on this particular celebration, on this particular Sunday or feast day. It is not meant to be a mini-homily or a preview of the day's Scripture readings.

The penitential rite calls the assembly to a sense of honesty: We are sinners all, who look for the mercy of God and find it here, with each other, in the Eucharist. The penitential rite might take the form of the "I confess to almighty God" with the three-fold Kyries or a series of invocations addressed to Jesus Christ, for example, "You were sent to heal the contrite: Lord, have mercy." This form of the penitential rite is not meant to be a personal confession of faults and failings as in individual reconciliation. Rather, it is meant to be a communal *pro*fession of faith in the one who saves us from sin. Sometimes, especially during the Easter season, the blessing and sprinkling of holy water replaces the penitential rite. This is not a penitential act, as it was at the beginning of High Mass in the pre-Vatican II liturgy, but rather a memorial of our baptism. Why not welcome the refreshing droplets of water that celebrate our new birth in Jesus Christ?

The "Glory to God" is to be said or sung (preferably sung) on Sundays (except during Advent and Lent), solemnities, feasts, and solemn celebrations of the local church (for example, an ordination). This is the hymn of the angels, which we mortals dare to make our own.

The opening prayer of the Mass begins with the priest's invitation: "Let us pray." Notice that he doesn't say: "Let *me* pray." And then he pauses for some moments. No, he hasn't lost his place in the book. The priest's spoken or sung prayer is to follow some moments of silent prayer by all; then, the silent prayer of all the worshippers is gathered into a concise prayer that the priest offers in the name of all. The assembly voices its "Amen!" to express its approval of this essentially communal prayer and thus makes this entire prayer its own.

All of this has prepared us for the Liturgy of the Word. But the Liturgy of the Word is not a prelude to or preparation for the Liturgy of the Eucharist. Rather, the Liturgy of the Word and the Liturgy of the Eucharist are linked as two necessary parts of one celebration, one act of worship. The Scripture readings and the homily are not a secondary part of the Mass; they are not merely a preparation for receiving Jesus Christ in holy communion. Jesus Christ comes to us really and truly in the Liturgy of the Word and in the Liturgy of the Eucharist, though in different ways. The Second Vatican Council's *Constitution on the Sacred Liturgy* stated that Christ "is present in his Word, since it is he himself who speaks when the holy Scriptures are read in the Church." God nourishes us well at the two tables of God's holy word and life-giving sacrament.

In the pre-Vatican II liturgy, the Scripture readings—an epistle and a gospel—for the Sundays and feast days were unchanging. But the years before the council had seen an increasing awareness that the Bible was the people's book and the liturgy was the people's work. Thus, the Fathers of the Second Vatican Council decreed that in the eucharistic liturgy "the treasures of the Bible are to be opened up more lavishly, so that a richer share in God's word may be provided for the faithful. In this way a more representative portion of holy Scripture will be read to the people in the course of a prescribed number of years." (*Constitution on the Sacred Liturgy*, no. 51)

The Council left this task to the commission responsible for the initial post-conciliar liturgical reforms. The working group entrusted with this work started at a logical and convenient point: the four Gospels. Matthew and Luke each provided enough Scripture passages for Sundays throughout the year; but Mark—the shortest Gospel—needed to be supplemented by readings from John. This is the heart of our present three-year cycle of readings: Year A, the year of Matthew; Year B, the year of Mark and John; and Year C, the Year of Luke. This arrangement enables us to see the living Christ through the differing lenses of the Gospel writers.

Once the gospel passages were selected, the revisers chose a first reading from the Hebrew Scriptures, one that would serve to shed light upon the teaching or work of Jesus in the gospel reading. Such a reading from the Hebrew Scriptures disappeared early in the history of the Roman eucharistic liturgy, and its return is very welcome. Many good stories and beautiful readings are now brought to the ears and hearts of Catholics. But it should not be forgotten that these readings from the Hebrew Scriptures are not merely preludes or "warm-ups" for what Jesus teaches or does in the gospel readings. For the Jewish people and for us, these readings are the word of God, God's self-communication, and thus filled with great spiritual truth in themselves. During the Easter season, a reading from the Acts of the Apostles replaces the reading from the Hebrew Scriptures. Here we glimpse the work of the risen Christ in the early community of believers, the same Christ who works in our church today.

After the first reading, a psalm has been selected to serve as a response to what we have heard. That is why this psalm is called "responsorial," and also because the assembly joins in on the response or refrain after the cantor or choir sings the verses. The refrain reflects and highlights an important aspect of the word that has been proclaimed. These refrains can stay in our heads all week long to shape our daily prayer.

The second reading on Sundays and solemnities (the greatest celebrations in the liturgical calendar) is usually from one of the letters in the New Testament. Here we find the apostles writing heartfelt messages to their early converts: encouraging them, instructing them, sometimes correcting them. We are centuries away from these early Christians in time, but often we are very close to them in their struggles to live the Christian faith. Thus, the second reading at the Eucharist can be a source of great spiritual value for us, especially if it becomes a subject for the homily.

The Gospel Acclamation is like the assembly's joyful salute to Jesus Christ, the very source of our faith. We stand for the proclamation of the gospel in respect and reverence for the Lord Jesus who speaks to us in these words. Even the book from which the gospel is proclaimed may receive special marks of honor:

Candles and incense are two ancient ways to honor Christ present in his word.

The homily has long been part of the Eucharist, but how long it should be remains hotly contested. About the year 150, St. Justin Martyr explained that "when the lector has finished, the president addresses us and exhorts us to imitate the splendid things we have heard." (Deiss 93) What a marvelous description of the preaching task that was the president's—the bishop's—in his day.

The Nicene Creed is a latecomer to the Roman eucharistic liturgy; it didn't find a place there until the year 1014. It might be seen as a response to all that has been said and heard and sung and prayed and preached in the Liturgy of the Word, as a proclamation of baptismal faith, the faith that leads us to share the Liturgy of the Eucharist that follows. But we should not forget that the great Eucharistic Prayer is the greatest statement of the church's faith.

St. Justin noted that intercessory prayer was a regular part of the Sunday Eucharist in his day, telling us that after the Scripture readings and the homily, "we all stand and pray." (Deiss 93) Today, in the "general intercessions" or "prayer of the faithful," we claim for people in need the salvation that Jesus came to give them by his life, death, and resurrection. We join our prayers to the powerful prayers of Christ; we pray *with* Christ and *through* Christ. The Spirit of God prays in our spirit as we offer prayers of intercession for the church, for civil authorities, for those oppressed by various needs, and for ourselves. And the faith that leads us to intercessory prayer at the Eucharist must lead us to alleviate human need outside it.

Liturgy of the Eucharist: Eucharistic Prayer

Then, Justin says, "bread, wine and water are brought up." (Deiss 93) And so they are today, in the procession with the gifts that was restored to the Roman liturgy after Vatican II. We bring forward bread and wine, and also the assembly's monetary offerings, things through which God will work in our midst; we do not bring forward symbols of our identity (for example, our team's jersey) or of our interests (for example, a football). Then, Justin says, "the president prays according to his ability and the people give their assent with an 'Amen!' " (Deiss 93)

Here we glimpse a very ancient and simple version of what we do in the Eucharistic Prayer, our prayer of praise and thanksgiving at Mass. Justin doesn't give us the actual words that the presider uses, but about sixty-five years later, we find that the Eucharistic Prayer is filled with thanksgiving for God's marvelous deeds in creation and redemption, and especially for the salvation that Jesus Christ won for us by his dying and rising. For Justin and for every community of believers down through the centuries, the Eucharistic Prayer is our most important way to remember and celebrate what God has done for us in Christ.

At the Last Supper, Jesus gave us a way to remember him. He gave us a meal to remember him by: the Eucharist, our thanksgiving dinner in his memory. When we, his disciples, share bread and wine in memory of Jesus Christ, that bread and wine become his Body and Blood; they become living signs of the new and everlasting covenant that God has made with us. When we share the bread of life and the cup of salvation, we know that the Lord Jesus is with us in this sign of his self-giving unto death.

The Eucharistic Prayer makes our celebration a remembrance meal, a memorial meal. When we share the Body and Blood of Christ in his memory, we are really remembering and celebrating everything that Jesus did, and taught, and suffered for our salvation until he comes again in glory. This memory is the heart of all we say and do during the Eucharistic Prayer. We remember the past saving deeds of God the Father in Jesus Christ; we celebrate our present life in Christ as his sisters and brothers; and we look forward to the day when we will share in God's eternal banquet of love. In the Eucharistic Prayer we recall and celebrate the past, present and future salvation that Christ has won for us.

The Eucharistic Prayer is the center and highpoint of our entire celebration. It is made up of different parts, but they form a single, unified prayer of thanksgiving and praise. The Eucharistic Prayer begins with the preface and its opening dialogue between the priest and the other members of the assembly. In the name of the entire assembly, the priest praises God the Father and gives thanks for the work of salvation, especially for some aspect of it in keeping with the day, feast, or season. The preface is like a short summary of what we are celebrating on a particular day. At its conclusion, we dare to join the angels in their hymn of praise and sing "Holy, Holy, Holy ... ." As far as I know, they don't mind us singing along.

Next comes the *epiclesis*, a Greek word for the invoking of the Holy Spirit upon the bread and wine. The assembly asks God to send the Holy Spirit so that our gifts may be changed into the holy Body and Blood of Jesus Christ. We ask the Spirit to do what the Spirit did in making the Word become flesh in the womb of the Blessed Virgin Mary.

Then follows the brief account of Jesus' words and actions with bread and wine at the Last Supper. Now, as then, Jesus gives himself to his disciples under the appearances of bread and wine to be their food and drink. Jesus Christ becomes really present in our midst as we do what he told us to do in his memory.

And so we proclaim aloud our faith immediately after the words of consecration in the memorial acclamation. In fulfillment of the command received from Jesus Christ through the apostles, we keep him in memory, we remember him as no one else, by recalling his passion, death, resurrection, and ascension. Every one of the thirteen approved Eucharistic Prayers has a section recalling the saving deeds of Jesus Christ. Listen closely for them at the next Eucharist in which you participate.

Next we offer to God our Father what God has given to us, the one and only perfect sacrifice: the sacrifice of God's beloved Son on the cross. His self-giving unto death and his rising from the tomb comprise a single, unique event that can never be repeated. But in the Eucharist, that once-for-all event is liturgically and sacramentally commemorated and made present to us. As we say in one of the prefaces: "Christ has given us this memorial of his passion to bring us its saving power until the end of time." (Preface of the Holy Eucharist II) Through the liturgy's words and actions, the whole of God's saving work in Christ is remembered, contained, and presented to us. That work becomes a present and living reality every time we celebrate the Eucharist. And this is what the church, and particularly the church here and now assembled, offers to the Father. Christ offers himself with us as his Body; we offer ourselves with Christ as our head. Christ takes the church into his own once-for-all sacrifice through the power of the Holy Spirit. In this way, the Spirit draws us into ever more perfect union with the Father and each other as the Body of Christ.

Then follow some intercessions: for our pope, our bishop, the clergy, and all God's people. Mentioning them here makes it clear that we celebrate the Eucharist in union with the whole church on earth and even in heaven. Because the church is larger than the community of believers on earth, we remember the saints who have gone before us, and we pray for those who have passed from this life to eternal life. Thus, we show that our offering is made for all the members of the church, living and dead, for all those who are called to share in the life promised by the Eucharist.

The last part of the Eucharistic Prayer is the doxology, pure praise. It is like a sacred toast to God the Father, through Jesus Christ, in the unifying love of the Holy Spirit. Our "Amen!" is our response to this sacred toast. One Sunday morning, as the assembly and choir were concluding the sung "Amen" to the Eucharistic

Prayer, a youngster burst into loudest applause. His enthusiastic participation in what was happening stopped me right there at the altar for a moment. I thought to myself: "This is what the Great Amen should do for us. It's like our applause for the marvelous deeds that God has accomplished for us in Christ." Our "Amen!" is meant to be our resounding affirmation of our faith prayed aloud in the great Eucharistic Prayer.

Is the Eucharistic Prayer the prayer of all the worshippers? Only the priest prays it aloud, after all. But this prayer of praise and thanksgiving is everyone's prayer. The priest offers this prayer with and in the name of the assembly. He speaks aloud the praise and thanks that are in our hearts. Our church has rediscovered the truth that, in the liturgy, it is really the whole Body of Christ that acts. Christ, our head, and we, his brothers and sisters, together offer praise and thanks to our Father in the Eucharist. This is how we are most clearly seen and heard to be the Body of Christ.

This is why the acclamations in the Eucharistic Prayer—the "Holy, Holy," the memorial acclamation, and the Great Amen—are so important. They help us to make this prayer our own. The three Eucharistic Prayers for Masses with Children are punctuated by acclamations that keep the younger (and older) worshippers attentive. The enthusiasm we bring to the responses and acclamations of the Eucharistic Prayer is an essential part of our active participation. And our participation in the acclamations is made easier for us when they are sung in true acclamatory fashion.

Someone has said that the priest should practice praying the Eucharistic Prayer aloud until he weeps. Why? Maybe until tears of joy fill his eyes at the thought of God's marvelous love for us in Jesus Christ. And maybe tears of sorrow at the thought of how much ingratitude still fills our hearts.

Almost forty years ago, Dag Hammarskjöld, the secretary general of the United Nations, was on a UN peace mission to central Africa. A plane crash claimed his life. He left behind, in his apartment in New York, a stack of about two hundred typed pages held in a clipboard, marked "personal." The pages turned out to be a diary of about 600 entries. This diary, later published as *Markings*, recounts Hammarskjöld's groping journey into Christian faith. In spite of his doubts, he was able to say "yes" to life and to God. One brief but powerful entry from his diary is: "For all that has been, thanks. For all that will be, yes."

We say this together at the table of the Lord. The Eucharistic Prayer invites us to say and mean these words: "For all that has been *in Christ*, thanks. For all that will be in him, yes." Yes, Amen. Thanks be to God. And only when we have learned to say thanks throughout our lives, only then, can we say and dare we say: "For all that will be, yes." Saying "Amen," "yes," to God's will for our lives as Jesus did, "thy will be done," is so much easier once we are used to giving thanks.

Liturgy of the Eucharist: Communion Rite

There have been many gifts of liturgical renewal over the past decades, since the promulgation of the *Constitution on the Sacred Liturgy* at the Second Vatican Council. One that we can all attest to is the wealth of new liturgical music that we have seen and sung during these years. And some of the most beautiful of this music has been composed for the communion rite. Our new liturgical music expresses for us the very best of our beliefs about the Eucharist we share.

In 1976, for instance, Omer Westendorff composed an original piece of music for the Forty-First Eucharistic Congress in Philadelphia. "Gift of Finest Wheat" has become a standard in parishes across our country. What lovely words it contains:

> The myst'ry of your presence, Lord,
> No mortal tongue can tell:
> Whom all the world cannot contain
> Comes in our hearts to dwell.
>> (Copyright permission obtained, Archdiocese of Philadelphia, 1977. All rights reserved.)

What a wonderful expression of both the awesomeness and intimacy of God's love for us in Jesus Christ and in the gift of the Eucharist. It is the mystery of this presence that becomes ours in the communion rite. It is the mystery of this presence that we are called to make real in our lives, just as it becomes real in and through the eucharistic bread and wine.

The music of Jacques Berthier and the Taizé community in France is sung in many parishes. In the popular "Eat This Bread," we sing:

> Eat this bread, drink this cup,
> come to me and never be hungry.
> Eat this bread, drink this cup,
> trust in me and you will not thirst.

Most obvious of all, we believe that the Eucharist is not a *thing*; the Eucharist is a *person*. The Eucharist is the Body and Blood of the risen Christ. Not "come to it" but "come to me" is what we believe and what we do in the communion rite. Christ lives and we share his risen life in his Body and Blood. And thus it is not we who live, but Christ who lives in us—as St. Paul said. What we share in holy communion is not a "what" but a "who": the person, Jesus Christ himself.

The eucharistic presence of Christ is a *personal* presence, not the impact of a cosmic force or the appeal of a captivating idea. Christ's "real presence" in the Eucharist is not based on our own wishful thinking or vivid imagination or divine magic. Christ is really present because of his promise to be with us always, both in his Body and Blood and in the assembly that shares them in his memory. Christ comes to us in the Eucharist to bring us the life coming from his saving death and resurrection. In the Eucharist we meet the living Christ just as truly, though in a different way, as if we had walked with him on this earth. Jesus Christ becomes personally and really present to and in his community of believers for our spiritual nourishment. His sacramental presence in the Eucharist is no less a "real presence" than his physical presence was. The "Amen" that we speak as we receive communion testifies to our faith in the Body and Blood of Christ present under the forms of bread and wine as well as our faith in the Body of Christ alive in each other.

Because Christ's presence is a personal presence, it creates a personal relationship between him and us. By sharing his Body and Blood, we are joined with Christ and with each other in the closest possible way. "Those who eat my flesh and drink my blood abide in me, and I in them," Jesus told us. (Jn 6:56)[11] As we share Christ's Body and Blood, we become members of that Body. This makes *us* part of the "real presence" of Christ as we celebrate the Eucharist.

The communion rite begins with the Lord's Prayer sung or said by all. In this prayer, which has been called a summary of the whole Gospel, we ask for our daily bread, the bread of the Eucharist. There follows a prayer for peace: not the peace the world gives, but the peace and reconciliation only Christ can give. We ask to be renewed in a spirit of love and unity before we approach the table of the Lord. Our sharing of a sign of peace puts our seal on the words we have prayed. This gesture is different from our introducing ourselves and welcoming each other before the liturgy begins. Here, right before we receive Jesus Christ in holy communion, we extend peace from on high throughout the assembly.

As the bread is broken and the wine poured out for communion, we remember through visual signs and gestures that the Lord Jesus was broken for us, his Blood was poured out for us. Breaking loaves of substantial bread and pouring out a generous amount of good wine helps us to know the lavish generosity of God in this sacred meal. And then we, God's holy people, are ready to come to the table and receive God's holy gifts, the Body and Blood of God's Son.

Our eating and drinking together makes this a meal of unity. No matter what our differences of race, age, background, size and shape, we become the one Body of Christ through our sharing of the one bread and the one cup. It was the desire to foster this essential experience of unity that gave rise to the welcome service of laypersons as extraordinary ministers of holy communion. Since the early decades of the last century, more and more people have been receiving communion at every Mass. As a result, people in the front of the church did not feel truly "one at the table" with those in the back of the church, and vice versa. Priests often felt hurried in giving communion, and the danger was that the experience could become less personal, less reverent, less intimate. Extraordinary ministers of holy communion help deepen the sense of unity in the communion procession. Some parishes have adopted another practice in this regard: All the members of the assembly remain standing until everyone has received communion. This posture of standing, a resurrection posture, unites the assembly as they receive the Body and Blood of the risen Lord. Of course those who can't stand that long sit down, but remaining standing is a powerful way of showing that we are one as we eat and drink together.

Drink together. We take the cup into our hands and drink the Blood beyond all price. We do not dip the consecrated bread into the cup of wine. Jesus said: "Take and drink," not "Take and dip." It is true that Jesus Christ is received whole and entire under the form of bread alone. But communion from the cup is allowed and encouraged at every Mass in order to highlight the sense of Eucharist as a meal, and we know that a meal is both eating and drinking. Holy communion has a more complete form as a sign when it is received under the forms of both bread and wine. And by drinking from a common cup—not from a small, individual cup—we show that we are united with God and each other in this bond of life and love.

The Eucharist is not only a meal; it is the richest of meals, the most satisfying of meals, the banquet of God's reign. It is not fast-food, with us running in and out, only halfway interested in what we are eating or who we are eating with, more concerned about what we've just come from or what we're going to do next. The Eucharist is a banquet in which the sacred food we share and the holy people we share it with are all that matter because it is really *Christ* who matters. We eat of the one bread and we become one in Christ. In this eating and drinking we become living and joyful members of the Body of Christ, one in the love we receive, one in the love we are to give. Composer Thomas Porter captures this so well:

> Let us be bread, blessed by the Lord,
> broken and shared, life for the world.
> Let us be wine, love freely poured.
> Let us be one in the Lord.

As youngsters would say, "This is totally awesome!" And so it is. After we have received Jesus Christ in holy communion, song or silence invites us to praise and thank God for the gift of Christ's Body and Blood. This is not a time for preparing to leave church (for example buttoning up our coats or gathering our belongings); rather, it is a God-given opportunity to prepare ourselves, by prayer and reflection, for living the Mass in our daily lives. Our prayerful silence at this time will help our fellow worshippers to enjoy the same. Then the priest's prayer after communion, spoken in the name of all, asks that our receiving of the Body and Blood of Christ may bear fruit in daily life and in eternity. In one way or another, the "why" of Christ's real presence and work in the Eucharist is reflected in these prayers after communion. They all testify that God's gift of love in the

Eucharist becomes our obligation to share that love with others outside.

Looking for the Perfect Communicant

Its bouquet hinted of roses, its color was deep ruby, and its aftertaste was slightly sweet—the kind of wine that would enhance any altar. Such was the judgment of the clerical sippers at the Third International Seminar on Altar Wine, held May 16, 1992 at Cocconato d'Asti in northern Italy. Here the wine, *Malvaxia Sincerum*, a local entry of Italy's Piedmont region, was deemed the best of a dozen products to grace the palates of the four elderly priest-judges who served as the "religious tasting commission." The winning wine was the result of a three-year research project aimed at finding "the perfect altar wine."

So now you know what the perfect Mass wine is like. Why all this attention given to wine? Because the fruit of the vine becomes the cup of salvation, the Blood of Christ. That transformation is at the heart of the mystery we celebrate in the Eucharist. But what about the perfect *receiver* of the consecrated wine? What are the characteristics of the ideal eucharistic communicant?

First of all, the perfect communicant is *prayerful*. The perfect communicant delights in doing what Jesus Christ, our high priest, made possible and makes possible now: worship of the living God. (Heb 9:14)[12] The perfect communicant delights in taking an active part in the liturgy of the church, while not neglecting personal prayer and communal prayer outside it. The perfect communicant delights to "call on the name of the Lord" (Ps 116:13)[13] in every need, for all in need.

The perfect communicant is *thankful*. Thankful for *all*: for all the joys that enlarge our spirits; for all the sorrows that seem to bring us low but then somehow raise us up with new strength; for health that enables us to grow and mature and work and play and learn and worship; for sickness that helps us see what really matters in life: our caring relationships with others; for abundance of all that sustains and enhances our human lives; for the scarcity that makes us one with our needy sisters and brothers. For *all* of this, receiving the Eucharist bids us say: "Thanks be to God!" There is no better way to do this than receiving communion with a grateful heart. Such is the "sacrifice of thanksgiving" that God delights in.

The perfect communicant is a *hearer and doer of God's word*. The Israelites told Moses, "We will do everything that the Lord has told us." (Ex 24:3)[14] Their history showed that their actions often didn't match their words. The same God who spoke to them long ago now speaks to us through God's word in the Scriptures. God's Word nourishes us just as truly, although in a different way, as the eucharistic bread and wine. The Liturgy of the Word and the Liturgy of the Eucharist together form one eucharistic banquet for our enjoyment. To receive the Body and Blood of Christ in holy communion is to recommit ourselves to hearing his word and living as he taught. It is to say and mean these words: "We will do everything that the Lord has told us."

It's true that the perfect communicant may be difficult to find, just like the perfect altar wine, *Malvaxia Sincerum*. That winning wine, not currently being marketed, remains more as a "point of reference" for other sacramental-wine producers. And indeed, the laudable characteristics of the perfect communicant are points of reference for our own reception of communion, an ideal to aim at. Receiving communion is something we grow into, something we shape ourselves into as it shapes us. Like a fine wine, our receiving of communion is brought to perfection over time, enriched by experience, and savored as a source of joy in the Lord.

There won't be any international competition for the perfect communicant as there was for the perfect altar wine. The perfect communicant wouldn't want or need such a mark of honor. Such a person knows that the invitation to receive the Body and Blood of Christ is a gift from God. To receive communion humbly, reverently, and gratefully is its own reward, a reward beyond all price. It is one of God's ways of shaping us into the likeness of Jesus Christ, whose self-giving unto death remains the pattern for our own.

Liturgy of the Eucharist: Sending Forth

Do you have announcements at your parish Masses? Surely you have a collection. What about announcements? Lots of them? Some people hate announcements at Mass, but when they have something that they want announced, they change their minds. The announcements, if any, are to follow the prayer after communion. This is a good place for them. Announcements often concern events in the life of the church or the parish, situations in the lives of those close by and far away. These events and situations call us to bring the power of the Eucharist to our daily lives: at home, at school, in the workplace, in the local community.

The love that we receive at God's table is not meant only for us gathered there. Our communion in the Body and Blood of Christ requires us to serve others as he did—throughout life, even unto death. As we receive Christ's gift of love in the Eucharist, we are to proclaim the saving power of his death by becoming one with him in his sacrifice. Then our lives will reveal a love that comes from the heart of Jesus, filling our hearts with unspeakable joy but also reaching others in need through us. In *our* dying to self, we find our true and necessary strength in the Eucharist. As we become truly eucharistic people, our love for the Body of Christ *in*side and *out*side our worshipping assembly will become one and endure forever.

The concluding rite of the Eucharist is the bridge between inside and outside. It is very brief; perhaps this stems from the days when persecuted Christians celebrating the Eucharist didn't linger any longer than necessary. But the brief parts of the concluding rite may be the most important of the Mass.

First, the blessing. As at the beginning of the Eucharist, so at the end we celebrate our faith in the Holy Trinity: Father, Son, and Holy Spirit. Their love has surrounded us from the beginning to the end of our worship, and it is their love we take with us as we leave.

We need God's blessing because in a sense our full, conscious, and active participation in the Eucharist is just beginning. Outside our assembly, our participation in the Eucharist must become service to others. There we must share our lives even as we have shared the Body and Blood of Christ. We may still feel a bit of physical hunger after receiving the morsel of consecrated bread and sip of wine in holy communion because the quantity of food that we receive is minimal. Can this not remind us that sharing these spiritual gifts commits us to providing for the physical needs of people less fortunate than ourselves? The broken bread tells us how our lives must be broken and given for others, for God's least ones. The wine poured out shows us how our lives must be poured out for the good of all. Thus, "Do this in memory of me" refers not just to the words and actions of our eucharistic celebration but also to the self-offering we are called to make in the power of that celebration.

Roman Catholics believe that the presence of Christ in the eucharistic bread and wine is not limited to the time when communion is shared in the assembly but that it endures even after. Thus, the unity in Christ that is effected by the Eucharist is also shared among the sick and homebound to whom communion is brought. Through this service of priests, deacons, and extraordinary ministers of holy communion, the sick and homebound are able to experience the saving presence of Christ just as the worshipping assembly does.

Only if we are sacrificing ourselves, pouring ourselves out for others Monday through Saturday, will our eucharistic sharing in church on Sunday be real for us. Only if we have tried to hear, really hear, the voice of God in the Sunday Scripture readings and in the circumstances of our daily lives during the week—only then will the word of God proclaimed and preached on in the Eucharist become God's word to us. And only if we have tried, really tried, to express love for our families and neighbors and even strangers, only if we have tried to be honest and considerate at work, to break down walls of oppression and to break through our walls of stubbornness, to share our gifts and talents in the service of others—only then will we begin to know what our full, conscious, and active participation in the Eucharist is and what it sends us to do. Filled with the blessing of God, we shall never go away empty.

But we do go away because, after the final blessing, we are dismissed by the priest or the deacon (by the deacon, that is, if the priest doesn't inadvertently steal his line). In the pre-Vatican II liturgy this was short and to the point: "*Ite, missa est.* Go, this is the dismissal." And from this "*missa,*" the Mass got its name. In those pre-Vatican II days, as now, some didn't hear the dismissal because they had left already. But the dismissal with our response, "Thanks be to God!" and the final hymn, are worth waiting for. Gathered by God into an assembly, having shared in God's praise and received God's gifts, we now are dismissed by God. We scatter out the doors to take up again our service of God and others in everyday life, praising the Lord who works in us and through us to help bring about God's reign on earth. We are meant to be the best demonstration, the best proof, of the life-giving power of the Eucharist because we *ourselves* become the Body of Christ that we have shared. We are to be the best witness to the power of the Eucharist by our love for Christ present on our altars and in our tabernacles as well as by our love for the members of his Body in this world. Go in peace. Serve the Lord. Serve his brothers and sisters as Christ serves you in the Eucharist. Thanks be to God.

Come, Holy Spirit

You listen attentively to the prayers of the Mass, don't you? Good. I thought you did. Like this prayer, for example:

> Lord, may the Spirit you promised
> lead us into all truth
> and reveal to us the full meaning of this sacrifice.

This prayer over the gifts for Pentecost Sunday is short on words but long on meaning. Truly it is one of the gems among the collection of Mass prayers, one of the best to come from the Holy Spirit. For the Spirit is the one who helps us to pray as we ought, both privately and publicly.

"May the Spirit you promised lead us into all truth." *All* truth. That's a big order, isn't it? Truth about God, the world, ourselves, the truth about how all of these and all of us are part of God's plan. That's a lot of truth! But the fundamental, all-important truth that the Holy Spirit reveals to us is this: "Jesus is Lord." Without the Spirit, no one can accept this truth or announce this truth or live this truth. But with the Spirit, we dare to make and rejoice to make bold proclamation of this truth: "Jesus is Lord."

"May your Spirit *lead* us into all truth," we pray. The Spirit does not coerce us, or force us, or bribe us into faith. The Spirit enlightens our minds and kindles our hearts and opens our ears, gently but powerfully, just as the Spirit did for the apostles on Pentecost. The Spirit leads us eagerly and strongly, just as parents lead their children along life's journey, giving hope and consolation along the way.

How does the Spirit lead us? By giving us abundant yet different gifts for living as Christians. These gifts are abundant yet different forms of service to each other, in Spirit-filled words and deeds of faith, hope and love for all to hear and see and rejoice in.

For every such word, every such deed proclaims the truth: "Jesus is Lord."

"Lord, may the Spirit you promised … reveal to us the full meaning of this sacrifice." What sacrifice? The sacrifice of Jesus on the cross, the sacrifice made present for us each time we celebrate the Eucharist. Each time we remember his death and resurrection by sharing his Body and Blood, his sacrifice becomes ours and our sacrifice becomes his. How? By sharing in Jesus' death to self, we find new life in serving others as he did.

Part of the "all truth" into which the Spirit leads us is this: The sacrifice of Christ must become *our* sacrifice. His life and death must become *our* life and death because we are the members of his Body in this world. That is the "full meaning of this sacrifice." But we grasp this truth little by little, with the Spirit's leading and guiding, over a lifetime. To be baptized into the one Body of Christ, to live as a member of that Body daily, is how we come to understand the "full meaning" of Christ's sacrifice and ours. We can't do that without the Spirit. But in every act of self-sacrificing service to others, we proclaim the truth: "Jesus is Lord."

The Eucharist, which we celebrate Sunday after Sunday, is the privileged place where we proclaim the truth: "Jesus is Lord." No one can hear the Scripture readings Sunday by Sunday and receive them as the word of God except in the Holy Spirit. No one can take those readings to heart and turn them into words and deeds of Christian living day by day except in the Holy Spirit. No one can look beyond the eucharistic bread and wine and see their Savior and their Lord except in the Holy Spirit. No one can speak or listen or care and serve as living and life-giving members of the Body of Christ except in the Holy Spirit. No one can let our songs of praise and petition echo in the heart except in the Holy Spirit. No one can be shaped into a member of Christ's Body through the words and actions and songs of our worship except in the Holy Spirit. That is part of the "full meaning of this sacrifice" that the Spirit reveals to us. And as we respond in the words and actions and songs of our worship, we proclaim the truth loud and clear for all to hear: "Jesus is Lord."

"Lord, may the Spirit you promised ...." The Holy Spirit, whom Jesus promised to his apostles, did come to them on Pentecost. That Spirit prompted them to proclaim the marvels that God had accomplished in the Lord Jesus. But that promised Spirit is ours today as we share in Christ's sacrifice. In the power of the Spirit, we celebrate the marvels God accomplished in Jesus, but also the marvels that God is accomplishing in us. For every one of those marvels, let us join God in proclaiming the truth: "Jesus is Lord."

Come to the Feast!

Once I was comfortably seated in a fast-food restaurant, successfully ignoring the high sodium and fat content of my meal, when I noticed a group of squirmy youngsters in a nearby booth. They obviously were awaiting (as patiently as they could) the return of whoever had seated them there before going to order their lunch. Soon their mother returned with a tray piled high with hamburgers, french fries, and soft drinks. The children's eyes lit up with joy and their mouths murmured their delight as the feast was set before them.

In the book of Proverbs, we are invited to a feast that is even more appetizing than this one. Wisdom, the divinely appointed hostess at this feast, makes a generous invitation to all: "Let [whoever] is simple turn in here; to whoever lacks understanding, I say, Come, eat of my food, and drink of the wine I have mixed!" (Prov 9:4-5)[15] Such is the lavish banquet of God's word that is set before God's people. The prophet Isaiah similarly invites all who are thirsty to come to the water and everyone who has no money to buy rich food and eat. This food and drink cannot be bought for money;

it is the freely offered word of God. This is the nourishment by which God's people advance along the way of understanding.

John the Evangelist describes Jesus as the divinely appointed host at the most lavish banquet of all: the feast of eternal life. Jesus is the Wisdom of God who gives food for eternal life to all who seek it. He is the revealer of God's truth, the divine teacher who has come to nourish all humanity with God's word. That truth is present in Jesus' word and in his flesh and Blood. Eternal life results from receiving that truth in two ways: by believing in Jesus' word, and by feeding on his flesh and drinking his Blood. What a life-giving feast is set before us!

And yet, as we receive the invitation to this feast, do not the hungry children in the fast-food restaurant put us to shame? How excited are we about sharing the feast of word and sacrament that God lavishly sets before us Sunday after Sunday? Various Church Fathers and popes have highlighted this twofold means of divine nourishment in Christ, which Vatican II's *Constitution on the Sacred Liturgy* calls "the table of God's word" (no. 51) and "the table of the Lord's body." (no. 48) God gives us a daily opportunity to receive this twofold presence of Christ: in the preached word and in the sacrament of the Eucharist. And yet, how unenthusiastic our response to this generous gift can be, how lifeless our reception of this pledge of eternal life.

That is why we need the Holy Spirit, the source and soul of all our prayer, to enliven our praise and thanksgiving. Only in the Spirit's power can we eagerly receive the bread from heaven and sing praise to the Lord with all our hearts for so great a gift: eternal life begun here and now, and brought to its promised fulfillment in the resurrection on the last day. Only in the Spirit's power can we give thanks to God the Father always and for everything, especially for the living bread and saving cup that we share in the Eucharist. And only in the Spirit's power can we share the gift of the Eucharist.

It is true that the riches of the Eucharist are limitless; Christ's infinite love for us insures that. Yet as with any meal, we can take away from the eucharistic banquet only as much as we are prepared to receive. A grateful heart increases our capacity for God's love. May the Holy Spirit give us a healthy appetite for the Lord's life-giving food.

A Primer on the Real Presence

In "Jesus Our Delight," a lovely translation of the 12th century hymn, *Jesu Dulcis Memoria,* poet Gerard Manley Hopkins celebrates the joy of those who savor the eucharistic presence of Christ: "To speak of that no tongue will do / Nor letters suit to spell it true; / But they can guess who have tasted of / What Jesus is and what is love."

Our human letters and words and sentences also fail us when we try to explain the "real presence" of Christ in the Eucharist. The results of a poll conducted in 1994 by the New York Times and CBS News may indicate some fuzzy thinking on the part of some Catholics. Fifty-one percent of weekly Mass-goers said they believe the bread and wine are strictly the "symbolic" presence of Christ. But the poll did not clarify what was meant by "symbolic" presence. Our Catholic faith teaches that the consecrated bread and wine are more than a visual aid to remember the passion and death of Jesus. Today's Catholics have a strong belief in Christ's eucharistic presence and some understanding of the "why's" of that presence, even if they can't explain all the "how's." That puts them in good company because generations of saintly theologians have labored long and hard to explain those "how's." If these teachers and preachers often disagreed about the "how's," they didn't believe any less in Christ's "real presence" as they tried to express the "why's."

For centuries the Roman Catholic Church has used the term "transubstantiation" to explain the change of the bread and wine into the Body and Blood of Christ. The Council of Trent (1545-1563) declared that this change was "most aptly" called "transubstantiation," thus acknowledging there were other descriptions of the change in the bread and wine. Like St. Thomas Aquinas before them, the Council Fathers strove to give a theological foundation to the reality of Christ's presence in the signs of bread and wine.

Outwardly, nothing is changed by the Lord's words of institution, "This is my Body," "This is my Blood." Inwardly, however, everything is changed. This inner change—the complete transformation of the bread and wine into the food of eternal life—is perceived only by the eye of faith. Our poor human gifts of bread and wine become the priceless gift of God's beloved Son. "Faith alone may safely guide us / where the senses cannot lead!" (*Pange Lingua Gloriosi*, hymn by St. Thomas Aquinas) This, I think, is what the humeral veil covering the Blessed Sacrament during the transfer to the altar of repose on Holy Thursday evening symbolizes for me. It reminds me that the eucharistic presence of Christ remains hidden, mysterious, beyond human knowing, not subject to human control or agendas or expectations. The God who took the initiative in saving us in Christ now takes the initiative in making Christ the Savior present to us in the Eucharist. There is mystery here, a mystery we do not and cannot control. But this mystery has the power to direct our thoughts and actions and lives in God's way, toward God's reign.

Transubstantiation remains one traditional and authoritative explanation of how Christ becomes present in the Eucharist under the forms of bread and wine. The "how's" of Christ's presence are mysterious, but the "why's" of his presence are less so. Perhaps as we seek words to describe some "how's" and "why's" of Christ's "real presence" in the Eucharist, we might use the letters of the word "p-r-e-s-e-n-c-e" itself.

Our spelling out of the basics of "real presence" begins with:

P = *personal*. The Eucharistic presence of Christ is a *personal* presence. God has rooted and grounded the church in the *person* of Jesus Christ, truly human and truly divine, not in any merely human system or institution or ideology. Thus, our faith in the "real presence" of Christ must be rooted and grounded in the person of Christ, the one who shares himself completely with us in the sacrament of his Body and Blood. Christ's "real presence" in the Eucharist is based on Christ's promise to be with us always, both in his Body and Blood and in the assembly that shares them in his memory.

Pope John Paul II wrote in his apostolic letter, *Mane Nobiscum Domine*: "Faith demands that we approach the Eucharist fully aware that we are approaching Christ himself." (no. 16) And he explained: "The Eucharist is a mystery of presence, the perfect fulfillment of Jesus' promise to remain with us until the end of the world." (no. 16)

R = *relational*. Because Christ's presence is a personal presence, it creates a personal relationship between him and us. In the fourth century, Cyril of Jerusalem explained to the newly baptized that Christ's "body has been bestowed on you in the form of bread, and his blood in the form of wine, so that by partaking Christ's body and blood you may share with him the same body and blood." (Yarnold 85) We eat of the one bread and we become one in Christ. We drink of the one cup and share in the wine that gladdens human hearts. In this eating and drinking we become the living and joyful members of the Body of Christ, one in the love we receive. The "real presence" of Christ is the whole Christ, head and members made one.

E = *eventful*, that is, filled with the saving *events* of Christ's life, death, and resurrection. The relationship with Christ that is ours through the Eucharist is based on a past event: the death of Jesus on the cross, into which we were baptized. (Rom 6:3) His self-giving unto death and his rising from the tomb is a unique event that can never be repeated. But in the Eucharist, that once-for-all event is liturgically commemorated: "Christ has given us this memorial of his passion to bring us its saving power until the end of time" as we proclaim in Preface of the Holy Eucharist II. Through the liturgy's words and actions, the whole of God's saving work in Christ is remembered, contained, and presented to us in his Body and Blood. That work becomes a present and living reality every time we celebrate the Eucharist.

The *Catechism of the Catholic Church* summarizes it this way: "The Eucharist is the memorial of Christ's Passover, that is, of the work of salvation accomplished by the life, death, and resurrection of Christ, a work made present by the liturgical action." (no. 1409) We don't get into a time machine and go back to the time of Jesus; God brings Christ's saving deeds into *our* time, our present, as we celebrate the Eucharist and receive holy communion.

S = *sacramental*. Jesus lived and died and rose to life again as a human being, in the midst of human beings like ourselves. At the Last Supper, Jesus was *physically* present. His disciples could see him and hear him and touch him in a way that is impossible for us after his ascension into heaven. Yet we shouldn't feel cheated. Today, in the Eucharist, Jesus is present under the sacramental signs of bread and wine. In this way, we are able to meet the living Christ *now* just as truly, though differently, as if we had walked with him on the roads in Galilee or the streets of Jerusalem. His sacramental presence in the Eucharist is no less a "real presence" than his physical presence was.

E = *especially*. In the eucharistic liturgy, Christ is "especially" present under the forms of bread and wine. So declared Pope Paul VI in his encyclical letter, *Mysterium Fidei* (1965). The Second Vatican Council's Constitution on the Sacred Liturgy (1963) stated the same thing. (no. 7). But both the Pope and the Council also identified other ways and places in which Christ is present: in the praying and singing assembly, in the ministry of the priest at the Eucharist, in the word of God proclaimed, in the sacraments.

Christ's presence "especially" in his Body and Blood does not mean "exclusively," for indeed "Christ is always present in his Church." *(Constitution on the Sacred Liturgy,* no. 7)

N = *nourishing* for our life in God. "In this great sacrament you feed your people and strengthen them in holiness, so that the [human family] may come to walk in the light of one faith, in one communion of love." (Preface of the Holy Eucharist II) The spiritual nourishment of the Eucharist is infinite if we are prepared to receive it. Like the hearth cake that the prophet Elijah ate in the wilderness (1 Kgs 19:4-9), the Eucharist strengthens us for our lifelong journey to God's presence in heaven. The Eucharist is nourishment for body, mind, heart, and soul—nourishment for our whole being, strength for our life of faith, for our journey of love. We Catholics cannot live without the Eucharist because in it and through it we are filled with all the life of God.

C = *community-building.* "By the fact of our receiving the sacred bread and wine, each of us becomes a room in the house where Christ dwells, that house being the Christian community." (O'Driscoll 108) In one way or another, this "why" of the "real presence" of Christ in the Eucharist is reflected in many of the Mass texts in the Sacramentary: for example, "Lord, may this eucharist accomplish in your Church the unity and peace it signifies" (Eleventh Sunday in Ordinary Time, Prayer after Communion); "May this sacrament of love be for us the sign of unity and the bond of charity" (Votive Mass of the Holy Eucharist, Prayer over the Gifts); "Lord, bring to perfection within us the communion we share in this sacrament." (Thirtieth Sunday in Ordinary Time, Prayer after Communion) Such prayers testify that God's gift of love in the Eucharist becomes our obligation to share that love with others outside it, especially the poor. Mother Teresa of Calcutta said: "The Eucharist and the poor we must never separate. ... If we really believe that he, Jesus, is in the appearance of bread and he, Jesus, is in the hungry, the naked, the sick, the lonely, unloved, the homeless, the helpless, the hopeless, then our lives will be more and more woven with this deep faith in Jesus, the Bread of Life to be eaten with and for the poor." In the Eucharist, we eat and drink together. We celebrate our unity in Christ, and we pray that we will always be one in the Christ we share. With all our differences of skin color, backgrounds, age, size, shape, tastes, and feelings, we become the one Body of Christ through our sharing of the one bread and the one cup. All of this is concisely but beautifully expressed in the alternative opening prayer for the solemnity of the Most Holy Body and Blood of Christ:

> Lord Jesus Christ,
> we worship you living among us
> in the sacrament of your body and blood.
>
> May we offer to our Father in heaven
> a solemn pledge of undivided love.
> May we offer to our brothers and sisters
> a life poured out in loving service of that kingdom
> where you live with the Father and the Holy Spirit,
> one God, for ever and ever.

E = *enduring*. We Roman Catholics believe that the presence of Christ in the eucharistic bread and wine is not limited to the time when communion is shared but that it endures even after. Thus, the community-building, which is effected by the Eucharist, also takes place among the sick and homebound to whom communion is brought. In this way they are able to experience the saving presence of Christ just as the worshipping assembly does. And the effects of receiving the Body and Blood of Christ endure even to the day of eternity: "How holy this feast in which Christ is our food; his passion is recalled; grace fills our hearts; and we receive a pledge of the glory to come, alleluia." (antiphon O *Sacrum Convivium*) The "real presence" of Christ in the Eucharist is the foretaste of his presence with us for all eternity.

Such are the letters that make up this primer of the "real presence" of Christ in the Eucharist, mere hints as to what his presence can be for us and in us. Such is our limited understanding of that presence in this life; in the life to come, our understanding will be turned into praise.

Eucharistic Adoration

In 1935, Father (later Monsignor) Ronald Knox published his book, *Heaven and Charing Cross: Sermons on the Eucharist*. In the sermon entitled, "Behind the Wall," Knox takes his text, a familiar one, from the Song of Songs: "Behold, he stands behind our wall, looking through the windows ... behold, my beloved speaks to me and says, Arise, make haste, my love ... my beautiful one, and come." (Cant 2:9,10)[16] Knox applies this text to the host in the monstrance, calling it "a kind of window through which a heavenly light streams into our world, a window giving access on a spiritual world outside our experience." At this window, "behind the wall of partition that is a wall of partition no longer, stands the Beloved himself, calling us out into the open. ... Arise (he says), make haste and come." And what does Knox hear Christ calling us to do?

> Come away from the blind pursuit of creatures, from all the plans your busy brain revolves for your present and future pleasures, from the frivolous distractions it clings to. Come away from the pettiness and the meanness of your everyday life, from the grudges, the jealousies, the unhealed enmities that set your imagination throbbing. Come away from the cares and solicitudes about the

morrow that seem so urgent, your heavy anxieties about the world's future and your own, so short either of them and so uncertain. Come away into the wilderness of prayer, where my love will follow you and my hand hold you; learn to live, with the innermost part of your soul, with all your secret aspirations, with all the centre of your hopes and cares, in that supernatural world which can be yours now, which must be yours hereafter.

In a sense, we are always peering into the mystery of the Eucharist, always peering into the meaning of its celebration and reservation and adoration. We peer over the shoulders of Saint Paul and Saint Ambrose, of Saint Augustine and Saint John Damascene, of Saint Thomas Aquinas and Juliana of Liège (the woman most responsible for the feast of Corpus Christi), of theologians and preachers and authors, of those women and men in our parishes and communities who seek to understand the eucharistic mystery by *living* it. With believers of all times and places, we are always trying to get a better glimpse, a deeper understanding, of what the Eucharist means. We are always looking at the history of the Eucharist: how the church has celebrated it and reserved it and adored it; at its theology: why we have done so and do so today; and pastoral practice: how we should do so today.

In his encyclical letter, *Mane Nobiscum Domine*, Pope John Paul II strongly encouraged adoration and prayer before the Blessed Sacrament. Such eucharistic devotions can deepen our sense of the holiness of the Eucharist, and also deepen our reverence for each other, the living members of the Body of Christ. Eucharistic adoration and prayer before the Blessed Sacrament celebrate the *present* of the *presence* of Christ. The "*present*" has two different senses:

1. gift: Christ's gift of self, his self-giving under the forms of bread and wine:
   - in his Body and Blood that we receive
   - in divine grace as we honor the Blessed Sacrament in prayer and adoration.
2. now: Christ's being-with-us now, just as really and truly as when he walked on this earth, but sacramentally.

The "*presence*" of Christ is a real Body and Blood presence. It is the mystery of Christ's being-with-us, a personal presence that leads to our adoration. I may feel awe in the presence of the Declaration of Independence, but I don't adore it. I do adore Christ the Lord present in the Blessed Sacrament. Pope Paul VI said that visits to the Blessed Sacrament "are a proof of gratitude, a pledge of love, a service of adoration owed to Christ the Lord there present." (*Mysterium Fidei*, no. 66)

The *present* (both the gift and the now-ness) of Christ's *presence* becomes ours in the Eucharist so that we can share the presence and gift of Christ with others. And eucharistic adoration can be a valuable means to help us receive and share his presence. Perhaps the document *Holy Communion & Worship of the Eucharist outside Mass* has this in mind when it states:

> Prayer before Christ the Lord sacramentally present extends the union with Christ that the faithful have reached in communion. It renews the covenant that in turn moves them to maintain by the way they live what they have received through faith and the sacrament. They should strive to lead their whole lives in the strength of this heavenly food, as sharers in the death and resurrection of the Lord. All should be eager to do good works and to please God, so that they may seek to imbue the world with

the Christian spirit and, in all things, even in the midst of human affairs, to become witnesses of Christ. (no. 81)

A Farewell Toast

Sometimes I wish I could design greeting cards; the people who do this seem so clever and creative, and so does their work. Take this card, for example, that portrays the Gospel story of the wedding at Cana. One of the waiters grandly announces: "Here's a better vintage that Jesus just provided." A thirsty guest reaches for a goblet with wine splashing out and says: "I'll try it." And when you open the card: "May God make this year better than any that's gone before. Happy Birthday!"

Have you ever wished that you could have been with Jesus, Mary, and the disciples at the wedding at Cana? Have you ever wondered what it might have been like to taste the marvelous vintage that Jesus provided to spare the newlyweds a social catastrophe?

Wonder of wonders, God works a greater miracle for us right now. God gives us an exquisite wine that we can't buy in any store, but God gives it to us for free. What is this wine, you ask? This wine is the Eucharist we celebrate.

God transforms our human words, songs, and gestures into something that pleases our God and lifts our spirits. The liturgy we celebrate is our human gifts transformed by God's power into a most powerful and refreshing wine. In the liturgy, God transforms our gifts of bread and wine into the Body and Blood of God's Son, but God also changes our lives into a living sacrifice of praise.

How does God do this? Through the ministry of generous women and men who assist us in our worship: the liturgical ministers of your parish who serve God and the assembly Sunday after Sunday and throughout the week. Through the words, songs, and gestures of their service, God transforms these human actions into something that gladdens our hearts as nothing else can.

This is the wine of which St. Paul said: "Be filled with the Spirit, addressing one another [in] psalms and hymns and inspired songs." (Eph 5:18b–19a)[17] The Holy Spirit, who transforms the bread and wine into the Body and Blood of Christ, transforms us into the members of his Body. As we worship, the human elements of our liturgy—our human words and actions—become divine praise.

But before this transformation can happen, we need to do what the waiters did at the wedding at Cana. They needed to draw the water as Jesus told them. And so do we. We need to fill ourselves with a certain "water": love for the word of God we hear in church and read at home; commitment to communal prayer in church and at home; looking at the material objects and outward signs of our worship and seeing God working through them for our salvation. Such is the necessary preparation for God's transforming action in the liturgy that results in our full, conscious, and active participation. When we are filled to our spiritual brim with such preparation for worship, the wine that God produces in our liturgy will be rich indeed.

This is how Jesus Christ satisfies our thirst for God's life and love: He gives us the wine of the liturgy to savor and enjoy. This is how Jesus Christ gives us now a foretaste of the wine God will serve on the final day, when the eternal feast of life and love will begin and never end. While we wait for that grand celebration, why not enjoy the Eucharist, right here and now? Take your glass and let God fill it with the overflowing love offered to us in our worship. To paraphrase the greeting card I described, "May God make your next celebration of the Eucharist better for you than any that's gone before."

Endnotes

1. *New American Bible with Revised New Testament.*
2. Ibid.
3. Paraphrased from *New American Bible with Revised New Testament.*
4. *New Revised Standard Version Bible.*
5. Ibid.
6. Ibid.
7. Ibid.
8. Paraphrased from the Douay-Rheims translation of the *Holy Bible.*
9. New Revised Standard Version Bible.
10. Ibid.
11. Ibid.
12. Ibid.
13. Ibid.
14. *New American Bible with Revised New Testament.*
15. Adapted from *New American Bible with Revised New Testament.*
16. Modernized from *The Holy Bible: An Abridgement and Rearrangement by Ronald A. Knox.*
17. *New American Bible with Revised New Testament.*

Bibliography

Catechism of the Catholic Church. Collegeville, Minn.: The Liturgical Press, 1994.

"Constitution on the Sacred Liturgy." *Documents on the Liturgy, 1963-1979*: Collegeville, Minn.: The Liturgical Press, 1982.

Deiss, Lucien. *Springtime of the Liturgy*. Translated by Matthew J. O'Connell. Collegeville, Minn.: The Liturgical Press, 1979.

Documents on the Liturgy, 1963-1979: Conciliar, Papal, and Curial Texts, English translation. Washington, D.C.: International Committee on English in the Liturgy, Inc., 1982.

Douay-Rheims translation of the *Holy Bible*. St Paul: E. M. Lohmann Co., 1911.

Eucharistic Prayer for Masses for Various Needs and Occasions. Collegeville, Minn.: The Liturgical Press, 1994.

Heidt, OSB, William G. *Inspiration, Canonicity, Texts, Versions, Hermenutics: A General Introduction to Sacred Scripture*. Collegeville, Minn.: The Liturgical Press, 1970.

"Holy Communion & Worship of the Eucharist outside Mass." *Documents on the Liturgy, 1963-1979*: Collegeville, Minn.: The Liturgical Press, 1982.

Knox, Ronald. *Heaven and Chäring Cross: Sermons on the Holy Eucharist*. London: Burns, Oates & Washbourne, Ltd., 1935.

Knox, Ronald. *The Holy Bible: An Abridgement and Rearrangement by Ronald A. Knox*. London: Sheed & Ward, 1938.

Kwatera, Michael. *Come to the Feast*. Collegeville, Minn.: The Liturgical Press, 2006.

Lutheran Book of Worship. © 1978. Augsburg Publishing House. Board of Publication, Lutheran Church in America, 1978.

"Mysterium Fidei." *Documents on the Liturgy, 1963-1979*: Collegeville, Minn.: The Liturgical Press, 1982.

New American Bible with Revised New Testament. Washington, D.C.: Confraternity of Christian Doctrine, 1986.

New Revised Standard Version Bible: Catholic Edition. Division of Christian Education of the National Council of the Churches of Christ in the United States of America, 1993.

O'Driscoll, Herbert. *A Year of the Lord.* Toronto, ON: Anglican Book Centre, 1986.

Pope John Paul II. *Mane Nobiscum Domine.* Vatican: Libreria Editrice Vaticana, 2004.

Roman Missal, The, English translation. Washington, D.C.: International Committee on English in the Liturgy, Inc., 1973.

Schroeder, OP, H. J., translator and editor. *The Canons and Decrees of the Council of Trent.* Rockford, Ill.: Tan Books and publishers, Inc., 1978.

Yarnold, SJ, Edward (editor). *The Awe-Inspiring Rites of Initiation: The Origins of the RCIA.* Slough, England: St. Paul Publications, 1971, Collegeville, Minn.: The Liturgical Press, 1994.